Minor Auto Body Repair

**ROBERT
DAN
HARMAN**

Minor Auto

Body Repair

CHILTON
BOOK
COMPANY
Radnor, Pennsylvania

Copyright © 1975 by Robert Dan Harman
First Edition   All Rights Reserved
Published in Radnor, Pa., by Chilton Book Company
and simultaneously in Don Mills, Ontario, Canada,
by Thomas Nelson & Sons, Ltd.

Designed by Carole L. DeCrescenzo
Manufactured in the United States of America

Library of Congress Cataloging in Publication Data

Harman, Robert Dan
  Minor auto body repair.

  Includes index.
  1. Automobiles — Bodies — Maintenance and repair —
Amateurs' manuals.   I. Title.
TL255.H35   628.2'6'028   76-915
ISBN 0-8019-6271-4
ISBN 0-8019-6272-2 pbk.

1234567890   4321098765

All photographs are by the author's wife, Lillian.

Dedicated to
My Mother and Father
Who Put So Many Good Things in
My Mind and Heart

Preface

This book was written by the shop foreman of an auto body repair shop located in a metropolitan area of Florida. This foreman has always felt sorry for the guy who works hard all week for his wages, and then because someone runs into his car in a parking lot and drives off, has to spend $50 to $100 of his pay to get his pride and joy looking like new again. He often thinks to himself that a person who can read and follow instructions, could fix his own car at home in the driveway with simple hand tools.

He wrote this step-by-step manual to guide the average American through the really simple process of minor collision damage repair. This book does not pretend to make a professional body man out of a bank clerk or try to convince a truck driver that he can repair a car involved in a head-on collision. However, if you can read, and comprehend what you read, there is no reason you can't repair minor dents in your car.

Furthermore, this book does not suggest that you try to paint the damaged area after you have fixed the dent. The painting side of body repair is very complex and requires highly specialized equipment. The painting portion of a light collision repair represents only about one-third of the final bill. If you get your dent fixed by following these simple instructions, you will have no problem getting a shop to do the painting. Of course, very small spots can be touched up with the factory duplicate touch-up paints which are available.

When it is all done, you'll know you did a good job when you show the results to your neighbor and he asks, "Where was it hit?"

Contents

Minor Auto Body Repair

Getting Started

Body Panels

First, let's talk a little bit about body panels. It makes no difference what panel, as hoods, doors, fenders and rear quarter panels are all the same when it comes to body repair. They are stamped into their shape in a press, and then spot welded to their inner reinforcement structures. When you make a dent in one, you stretch the metal. If you stretch it too far, it either requires a new panel or special equipment to repair it. The biggest mistake most do-it-yourselfers make is stretching the panel more, in trying to repair it, than it had been with the dent in it. As a result, they end up with a bulge instead of a dent. When you do this, you have twice the trouble you had when you had the dent, and if you don't have access to special equipment and some very special talent, you are in big trouble.

So let's make an agreement, you and I. I'll do my best to talk you through the repairs we're trying to make, but you must use common sense. If the job is too big or if the panel is stretched very badly, don't try to repair it and end up with a big mess.

What we're really trying to do here is help you with small repair jobs. Minor repairs have come into the shops where I've worked that I could have done blindfolded. In most cases, if it is a very big job, your insurance will cover it. O.K., so now we have agreed. We won't bite off more than we can chew.

Tools and Materials

The first thing to do is to assemble the tools you will need. They are inexpensive and readily available at most auto paint supply stores, discount stores, and mail order auto suppliers. One might think that for a small job on a door or fender, it would seem silly to buy any tools. Look at it this way. You probably have a claw hammer hanging in your garage or a quarter-inch drill with an assortment of

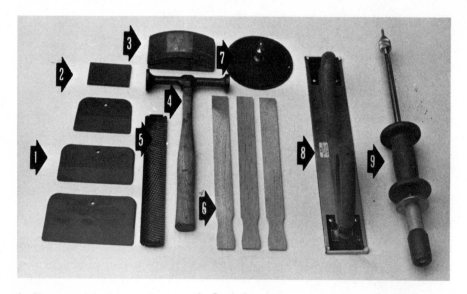

1	Three assorted spreaders	4	Body hammer	7	Grinding attachment
2	Glazing squeegee	5	Plastic file	8	Sanding board
3	Sanding block	6	Paint paddles	9	Dent puller

drills, etc., which you don't use every day of the week. So there is nothing wrong with having a few cheap body tools hanging that can pay for themselves time and again.

The basic tools for minor repair are as follows:

> Body hammer
> Dent puller
> Sanding board
> Sanding rubber block

¼ in. drill w/drill bits
Half round plastic file
Package of plastic spreaders
Putty squeegee
Grinder attachment for drill
Paint paddles

Materials you need for your first job:

1 quart auto body plastic, with tube of hardener
1 tube of glazing putty
1 can of aerosol lacquer base primer
2 5 in. grinding discs (24-grit), Used on drill
6 17 in. × 2⅔ in. sanding paper (36-grit), For sanding board
6 17 in. × 2⅔ in. sanding paper (80-grit), For sanding board
3 3¾ in. × 9 in. sanding paper (36-grit), For hand use
3 3¾ in. × 9 in. sanding paper (80-grit), For hand use
3 3¾ in. × 9 in. sanding paper (100-grit), For blocking
1 gallon lacquer thinner, For tool clean up

You won't use up all these materials on your first job, but they can be used at a later time. Put the lids and caps on them when

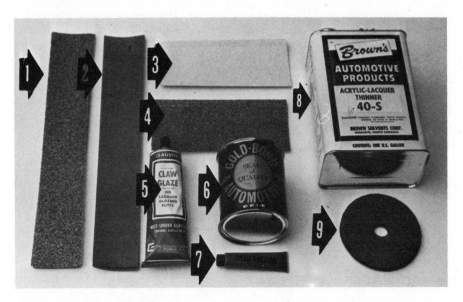

1	17 in. × 2⅔ in. sanding paper (36-grit)	5	Glazing putty
2	17 in. × 2⅔ in. sanding paper (80-grit)	6	Plastic filler
3	3¾ in. × 9 in. sanding paper (100-grit)	7	Hardener for plastic filler
4	3¾ in. × 9 in. sanding paper (36- and 80-grit)	8	Gallon of lacquer thinner
		9	5-in. grinding discs (24-grit)

you're through, and store them away for future use. Perhaps if you do a good job on your car, you'll be using them on your neighbor's car next week. Ever think of that? (Don't do it too cheaply though.)

CAUTION
MOST OF THE PRODUCTS YOU WILL BE USING CONTAIN HARMFUL CHEMICALS, SO BE EXTREMELY CAREFUL. ALWAYS READ THE COMPLETE LABEL BEFORE OPENING THE CONTAINERS. WHEN YOU PUT THEM AWAY FOR FUTURE USE, BE SURE THEY ARE OUT OF CHILDREN'S REACH!

Basic Method

Now you're ready to begin. All repairs discussed in this book involve more or less the same basic steps.

Study the Damage

Now, take a few minutes to study the damaged area. Try to visualize what shape or contour it had before it was damaged. If the damage is on the right fender, go around and look at the left fender. Study the lines of the panel, and then try to think the problem out. I've seen professional body men get into trouble on small jobs, because they started swinging a hammer before they studied the damage. There is no substitute for using your head.

If there is access to the back side of the panel so you can use a hammer to bring the panel back, fine. If not, you will have to bring it out the best you can from the outside. Until now, I haven't mentioned the most important tool a body man has, and that is the palm of his hand. By laying your hand, palm down and flat, on the panel, you can determine a lot of things you can't even see. You will see what I mean a little later.

Let's categorize the two types of repairs we will be making. The first are the door dings, stone dents, or in other words, dents that are so slight that there's no point in trying to metal finish them i.e., to bump them out. For dents that fall into this category, just grind the old finish back and fill them with plastic. Follow the steps at the end of the next category, beginning with, *Preparing the Panel for Plastic Filler.*

The second category is the one that requires the most care. As I mentioned before, this is where the novice can get into big trouble. Let's assume you have a fair size dent in your front fender. As you look at the damage, try to visualize how the damage was done. You might say to yourself, "The point of impact was here and the angle of impact was about thirty degrees to the rear." Try to figure how

Arrow shows good example of stress line. Pull or hammer out along this line.

the dent was actually made. In most cases, to repair it you follow
the reverse in pulling or hammering it out. Let's assume again that
you can get to the back side of the damage with a hammer or pry bar
and you begin working the metal back to its original position. Go
slowly. Work a little at a time. This is where the palm of your hand
is so very useful. When the dent is close to being back to its original
shape, lay your hand flat on the panel and slowly slide it back and
forth. Get your body behind your hand, and as you move your hand
across the panel, think where the highs and lows are. THINK
STRAIGHT. Be sure your hand is flat, as you can tell nothing by
feeling with your finger tips.

Using the Dent Puller
Quite frequently you'll find that there is no way to get behind a damaged panel. Now the dent puller comes into use. Study the panel
carefully and determine where the lowest spot is. This is usually the
best part to pull out first. Quite often there are stress lines in a damaged panel. Once you learn to read these, you will be well along in
learning sheet metal working. Stress lines usually run from the
lowest part of the damage toward the outside.

Using a ¼ in. drill and a drill bit about half the size of the end
on the dent puller, drill a series of holes along the stress lines to the
lowest place in the dent. Make a few trial pulls and carefully watch

Using the dent puller. On a small dent like this, be careful not to pull the metal out too far. Just a few light taps with the puller in each hole will suffice.

what the panel does. Since no two dents are the same, I can't actually tell you exactly where to make your pulls. If you watch what the panel is doing when you put tension on it, you can tell whether or not you are pulling in the right place. If it looks as if you should move over a few inches, drill more holes and try it. The important thing to remember is not to be in a hurry.

Later in the book, there is a series of step-by-step repairs to various panels. It may be helpful to compare one of these jobs with your own. I have used some of the more common repairs a body shop does. One of these should be close to your particular dent. The old adage is, however, if you see one dent, you've seen them all. They all come out the same way.

Working the Panel Out: Go Slowly Here

The important thing to remember, when working the panel back to its original shape, is not to push or pull it out too far. That is the reason I put so much importance on going slowly on the first couple of jobs. On a small area it is fairly easy to determine whether your damaged area is very close to its original shape by using the palm of your hand as I described before. If the area is quite large, however, such as the whole length of the panel, a trick used by a lot of body men is to take an ordinary yardstick and lay it flat across the repair area. Yardsticks, the kind you get from the hardware stores and lumber companies, are very flexible and will curve over just about any panel—including contoured ones. Lay the yardstick flat over

Using a yardstick to find highs and lows on a large area is an old body man's trick. Use it when straightening metal and when filling in with plastic.

the area and slide it up and down the panel. Watch the edge of the yardstick that is against the metal. High and low spots may now be seen very easily.

When you are finished bringing the panel out to its original position, low spots shouldn't be more than one quarter inch at the deepest point. There are shops that allow much more variation than that, and there are shops that insist that the panel be even closer than one quarter of an inch. If you don't get your panel close to original, the plastic filler will be much too thick. In a few months it will begin to crack and will have to be redone. I once had an old timer tell me when I first went to work for him, "I don't care if your plastic work is thick, just so it isn't deep." At any rate, keep the plastic as thin as you can. Plastic was designed to take the place of lead when it became too expensive and panels became too thin to be reshaped with heat. It was never intended to be used for filling large low spots.

Now, compare your work with some of the photos, and when you are satisfied that you are as close as you can get, then start with the second phase.

Preparing the Panel for Plastic Filler
Insert the grinder attachment into your ¼ in. drill and put on one of the 5-in. grinder discs. You should wear safety goggles. If you don't

have them, put on a pair of light shaded sun glasses. Most ¼ in.
drills don't turn at a dangerously high RPM, but the chips and dust
can very easily get into your eyes.

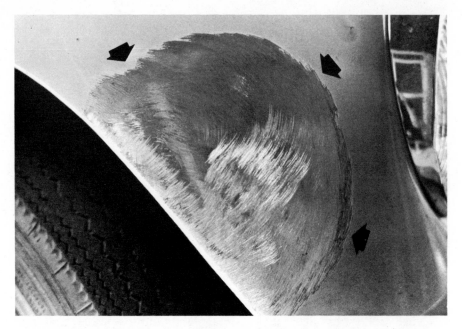

Arrows indicate how the old finish is ground back several inches from the damage. This gives everyone, both you and the painter, plenty of working room.

Grind the old finish off the damaged area. You will have a hard
time getting all the paint off in areas where you have done some
pulling, especially around holes you've drilled. Do the best you can.
If you have a wire brush for your drill, this sometimes does a good
job around such places and in other areas that are inaccessible. If
you are working around a bumper or chrome molding, it is a good
idea to put several layers of masking tape over them in case you
should slip during the grinding operation. This will also keep the
plastic, which can be very hard to get off, from getting on them.
Leave the tape on until you have completed the job.

As you grind back the old finish, be sure to go three or four
inches away from the damaged area, so that there won't be any
plastic on top of the old finish at the edges of your repaired area
when you're finished. When you take the car to the paint shop and
the painter looks at your work, there won't be any question in his
mind that you know what you're doing if there's no filler on top of
the paint. Plastic on top of the paint edge indicates an unprofes-
sional job. To explain this as simply as possible without getting into

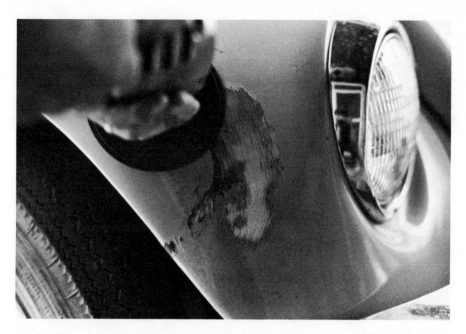

Using the ¼-in. drill with a grinding attachment. Always use safety precautions such as a three prong electrical plug and glasses.

the technical end of the painting process, if your plastic filler work goes out beyond the old paint edge, the finished panel will have an ugly ring showing right where the plastic starts and ends. If the painter has to work right up to the edge of your filler, there is always the chance of his getting low spots in your repair with his air sander. All the effort you made to get a perfect job will have been for nothing and you can't blame the paint shop.

Mixing and Applying the Plastic

Now we're ready to "mud" the panel. Make a mixing board out of a piece of cardboard box. Open your package of plastic spreaders and select the size that seems to fit the situation. I like the medium size myself, which is about five or six inches wide. Naturally for larger areas, you would use a larger spreader. After you have read the label on the can of filler, open the can. Using one of the paint paddles, remove enough material to apply a medium coat to the panel and put it on the mixing board. Apply the correct amount of hardener from the tube and thoroughly mix it. When using hardener, it is better to use too little than too much. This gives you more working time and less chance of getting lumps in the mixture.

As you first apply the plastic, take small amounts on your spreader and sort of wipe it into the metal. This insures that you will

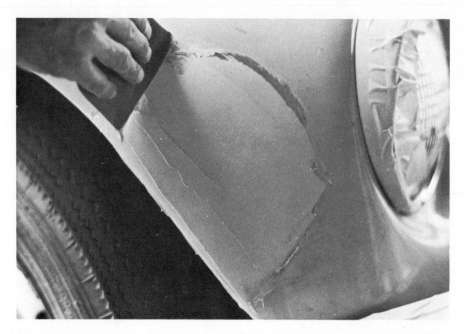

Spreading plastic is simple once you get the hang of it. Apply plastic smoothly and quickly, and then allow it to harden.

Mixing the hardener into the plastic takes practice because temperature and humidity determine how much hardener to use. Too little is better than too much.

Mix the plastic thoroughly before applying it to avoid soft spots in your work.

obtain good adhesion and is called *tinning* the metal. After the area is tinned, go ahead and spread the plastic in smooth, even strokes. This is important. Spread the material on as smoothly and as quickly as you can. When you have a fairly smooth coat, leave it to dry. As soon as the plastic turns to a solid state (about the consistency of

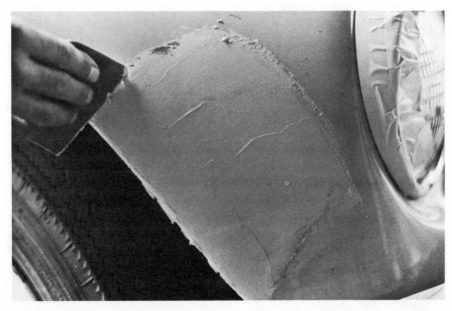

Learn to apply the plastic quickly. Once you get used to it, there is plenty of time to tin the metal with small amounts on your spreader.

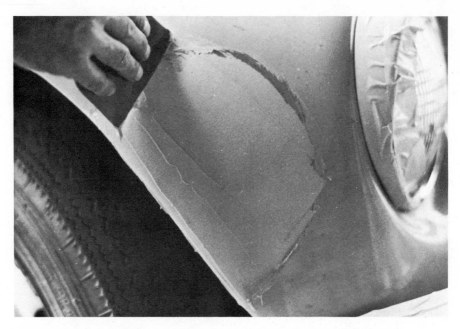

When making your final strokes, try to follow the contour of the panel. The smoother you apply the plastic, the easier the rest of your work will be.

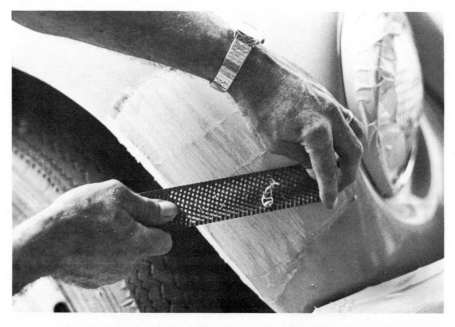

Remember to use the plastic file as soon as the plastic hardens to the consistency of rubber, if you wait too long to file, your work will be doubled.

soft rubber) take your plastic file and, very lightly, knock off any high spots. Don't file too heavily, though, as the file will dig in and pull the plastic loose from the metal. After you've done this, let it set up for about fifteen to thirty minutes, depending on the temperature and the amount of hardener you used. One word of caution here. Don't spread the plastic on and then go in to eat lunch, because when you come back, the filler will be hard as stone. If you don't work the plastic in stages as just explained, your labor will be doubled.

After the plastic has set for about half an hour, it is time to work it down with the sandpaper. If the area is very small, use the

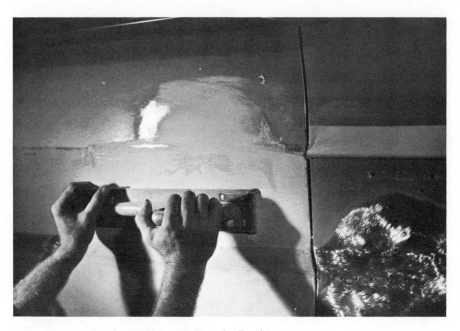

Using the sanding board to work the plastic down.

rubber block and a piece of 3¾ in. × 9 in. (36-grit). If it is large, use the sanding board and a piece of 17 in. × 3¾ in. (36-grit). Sand the plastic smooth, watching that you don't get the area too low. This is just the first coat so if you notice low spots and pin holes in the work, don't worry about it. When you first start sanding on fresh plastic, you will notice that the sandpaper tends to clog. Use a small knife or similar object to flick off the specks from time to time to keep the paper from completely filling up. After you have gotten the area to about the right height, wipe the panel with a clean rag and recoat it with another application of plastic. You will notice that this time the material will go on much smoother and you will have more control when spreading it. Just as before, get it smooth and then *leave it alone*. Repeat the procedure you used on the first coat with the file and then allow it to set up hard. Now, work the plastic down with a sanding block or sanding board to one sixteenth of an inch of the desired finished height.

Now, change your paper to the 80-grit and continue to work it down to the finished level. Knowing when to stop with the 36-grit and start with the 80-grit will come to you after a few times. The beauty of it all is that if you get too low with the 80-grit, you can always apply another coat. If you have trouble telling whether you are too low or too high by using the palm of your hand, grab the yardstick again and use it to spot the voids. It works just as well during this stage as it did when you were bumping out the panel. Usually a second or third coat on the damaged area is the standard for a good body man, but if it takes you five or six, don't worry about it. You're new at this.

I would like to insert a little bit of encouragement for your ego. I've had body men work for me that could never get a panel straight, no matter how many times they applied plastic. The important thing is to learn to read what the palm of your hand tells you as you run it over the panel.

THINK STRAIGHT. Running your hand back and forth rapidly over the panel, won't tell you a thing except that it isn't straight. Your hand will automatically tell your brain that it feels lumps and waves. Watch your hand as you move it slowly along the repair and concentrate on what is high and what is low. Let's say you're very close to having the panel perfect, I said close to having it perfect. It's a natural tendency to think that this is good enough, and when it is painted, it won't show. WRONG! Painting not only DOESN'T HIDE, IT HIGHLIGHTS DEFECTS.

This is where the amateur can often do a better job than a lot of body shops. Most body men work on a percentage of the total labor of every job; therefore, the quicker they finish one job, the quicker they can start another. If it is not perfect (just close), instead of "hitting it" one more time, they turn it over to the painter. Most body men know from experience how much they can get away with, and if the shop doesn't insist on perfect work, the customer gets a sloppy job. Since time should not be one of your motives, there is no excuse for anything but perfection.

Priming and Glazing

When you are sure the panel is straight, when it looks good and your hand tells you it is good, let's take one more step to insure it is

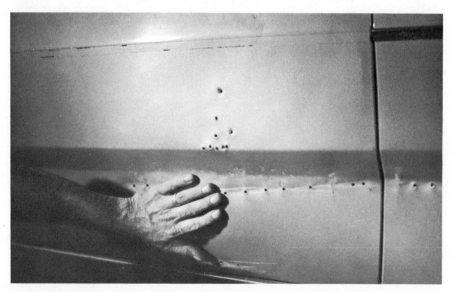

Learn to use the palm of your hand as a gauge. It's one of the body man's most important tools.

not only good, but perfect. Take a clean rag and wipe the panel clean. Now, shake the aerosol can of primer thoroughly as per the instructions on the label. Apply a medium coat of primer over the area you have just repaired. Be sure all the plastic is covered and just a few inches of the metal surrounding it. Don't go way out on

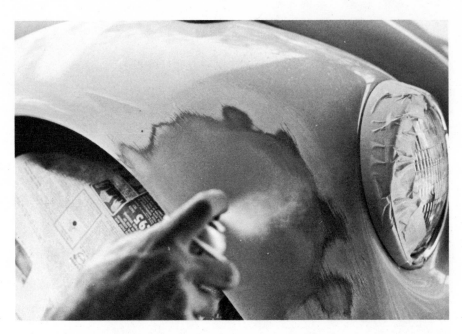

Allowing the first medium coat of primer to go way beyond the edge of the old finish just wastes material.

the metal and onto the old finish edge, as you will just be wasting material. Let the primer dry, usually thirty minutes is sufficient.

When the primer is dry, take the small rubber squeegee and the tube of glazing putty and apply a thin covering of putty over the repaired area. Apply this material smoothly and quickly. You will notice that if you go back over an area that you had puttied just seconds before, it will tear the film of the first application. This material must be put on in one stroke applications and then left to dry. In other words, squeeze about a tablespoon of putty onto the edge of the squeegee and immediately, with one quick stroke, apply it the length of the repaired area. If there is still some putty on the squeegee after the first pass, drop down and wipe it on right below the first pass. When you have the area covered, leave it to dry for about an hour.

Clean the squeegee at once with lacquer thinner and a rag. If it takes longer than an hour for the putty to dry, you probably put it on too thickly. The purpose of glazing putty is to fill sandpaper scratches, small low spots in your work, and pin holes in the plastic.

When the putty is dry, take a paint paddle and cut it to nine inches with a wood saw or a hack saw. Now, take a piece of 3¾ in. × 9 in. (100-grit) sandpaper, and fold it over the shortened paint paddle lengthwise. Lay the covered paint paddle flat on the puttied

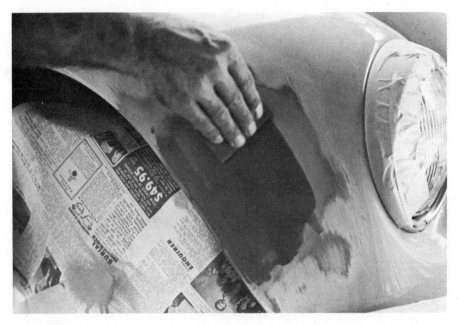

Apply glazing putty in one stroke applications. If you go over what you have already spread you will tear the previous application away from the surface.

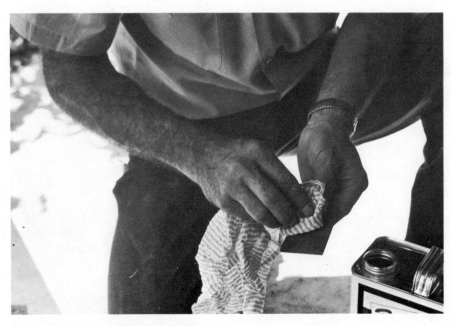

Lacquer thinner is the best for cleaning putty from your squeegee. Be careful with this liquid, though, as it is more flammable than gasoline.

Folding 100-grit paper
over shortened paint
paddle for use in blocking
glazing putty.

area and sand it down until it is smooth. When you finish sanding, there shouldn't be very much putty left on the panel, as it was only applied to fill sandpaper marks, pin holes and very minute low spots. You should see most of the primer that you previously applied. I like to think of putty as nothing but thick primer. In the old days of body repair, scratches and voids were filled by priming

After the putty has dried, block sand with the shortened paint paddle and 100-grit paper. This removes scratches and small low spots.

heavily and sanding, sometimes as many as five or six times. With glazing putty, you do the same thing in one operation. When you have finished sanding the area with the paint paddle and the 100-grit paper, take another piece of 100-grit paper and fold it in thirds lengthwise. With the folded paper in your palm, very lightly go over your work with long smooth strokes.

Finish sanding with a piece of 100-grit folded in thirds. Use long even strokes. Sand very lightly.

Don't sand in any one spot but in long strokes the entire length of the repaired area. If you dwell on one spot, you will lose everything you have gained and finish with a wavy job. Take a clean rag and thoroughly wipe the area. Now, get down close to your work and carefully inspect it. Look for any imperfections or pin holes that may still remain. If you see any bad spots, get the putty and squeegee out and do these spots individually, with just enough material to do the job. In other words, if you see a few pin holes, wipe the putty into the holes flush with the surface rather than put a big gob on and have to go through the blocking procedure again. These areas should dry in just a few minutes. When dry, sand them down smooth with 100-grit, being careful not to overdo it and damage the adjacent areas. Wipe the area down again and prime the entire area with a medium coat. When you apply the primer this time, prime over the old finished edge a couple of inches. This will prevent the metal from rusting until you get to the paint shop with it.

You and the Painter

Now is the time for you to scout up a good painter. Your best bet is to look in the Yellow Pages of your phone book and jot down two or three addresses of independent body shops. Don't bother going to any of the new car dealers, as they are always loaded with work, and probably wouldn't do your job.

One thing to remember when you ask about getting your paint work done: The people you are about to deal with are professionals in their field. They are always busy and are trying to make money. Use the humble approach, and don't try to make them think you are an old hand at their game. They'll find you out before you have said ten words. Simply tell them you have repaired the panel on your car and you would like them to refinish it. If they brush you off, thank them for their time and go to another shop. It will mean they have more work than they can handle. When you find a shop that will look at your panel, they will see you have done a good job and will give you a price.

This is the time to explain to them approximately where your repair starts and stops and tell them that you have ground the old finish well back from your plastic work so the painter can get hold of the edge and feather it back. Tell them you only lightly primed to prevent rust and you would appreciate the painter repriming it and sanding it before he paints it. Whatever you do, don't try to explain to them how the accident happened. Believe me, they aren't interested. I speak from experience. Don't brag about your work. If you did a good job, they'll know it.

Moldings and Trim

If any moldings or trim pieces were damaged, go to your dealer's parts department and talk to the parts man. Explain what you need and in most cases they will help you out. Most moldings are simple to put on. If you are careful and watch how the old ones come off, you should have no problem installing the replacements.

A Word about Rust

Having been born and raised in northern Indiana where the salt mines work overtime in the winter, I'm somewhat of an expert on rust repair. One thing that you must remember about a rust hole in a panel: If you grind off the area and fill it with plastic, you can be sure it will soon be back. All sorts of materials have been marketed to take care of rust temporarily, from plastic screen to aluminum tapes. They all serve the purpose for which they were designed, *temporary repairs*.

If you have a rust hole in a panel, there is only one way to repair it permanently and that is to weld in a new piece of sheet metal. If you don't have the tools to do this job, such as welding equipment, don't waste your time and money trying to patch it. Take it to a shop and have them weld in a piece. Then take it home and finish it the same as you would a dent. It will cost you a little more in the long run, but your money will have been well spent.

There are two reasons you can't do a good job without welding in a new piece of sheet metal. One, rust is a chemical reaction that will cause pressure under your work. That's where the blisters come from. Two, the back side of your panel (and your filler) is wide open to moisture and fillers that aren't painted are like a sponge. So if you have rust, get a patch welded in before you start applying that high-priced material.

Ten Key Steps to Easy Body Repair

1. Study the damage before you start.
2. Try to imagine how the damage was done.
3. Work the panel back to shape slowly. Take your time.
4. When grinding back the old finish, go far enough so that no plastic will be on the old finish when you're through.
5. Learn to use the palm of your hand. A good body man can't work without it.
6. Don't depend on paint to hide anything. If you can feel it, you will definitely see it when the job is done.
7. Glaze small imperfections in your plastic work—pin holes, scratches and very minor low spots with smooth quick strokes.
8. Block your glazing with the paint paddle and 100-grit sandpaper.
9. Prime lightly, covering all bare spots to prevent rust.
10. Remember, the painter is the professional. Don't try to fool him.

The following step-by-step repairs were done with the same tools you are using. The materials were bought in small amounts at retail prices in order to be honest and fair.

REPAIR 1
Small Fender Dent

A creased Volkswagen fender, a classic parking lot ding. Careless parkers will leave you little reminders like this of their thoughtlessness. Notice that the exposed, bare metal has already begun to rust. Let's get started.

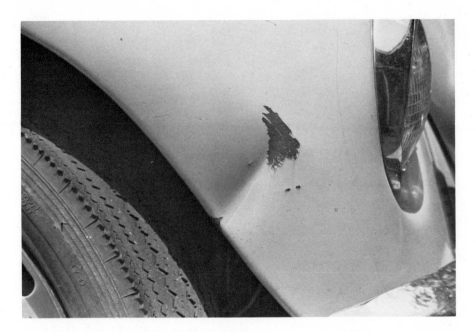

Step 1. Study the panel. Read the stress lines. A little thinking here can often save a lot of work.

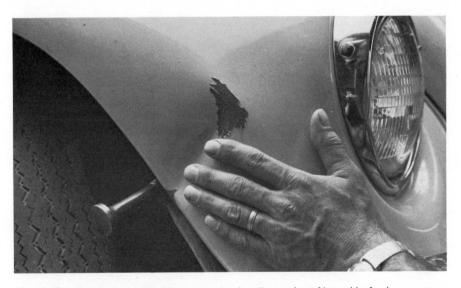

Step 2. Cautiously bump out the crease using the palm of hand to feel your way.

Step 3. Think straight!
As you move your
hand along the panel,
read what your palm is
telling you about the
surface.

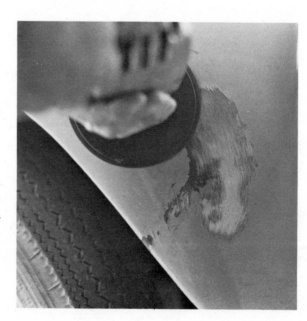

Step 4. Remove the
old finish with a drill
and grinding attach-
ment.

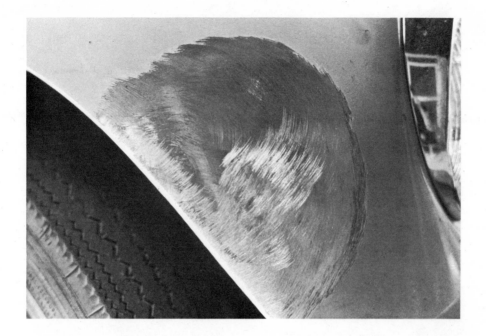

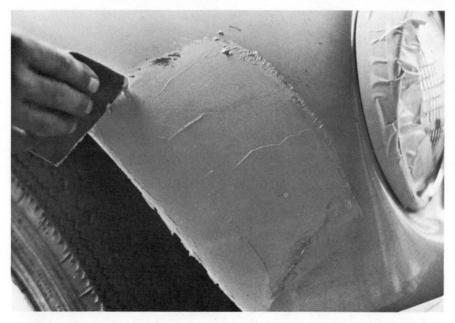

Step 5. When the panel is ground clean (above), apply plastic as quickly and as smoothly as possible (below).

Step 6. File the plastic before it gets too hard.

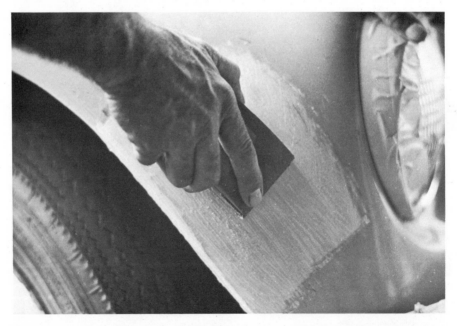

Step 7. Using a sanding block for small jobs or a sanding board for larger ones, work the plastic down to about the desired height.

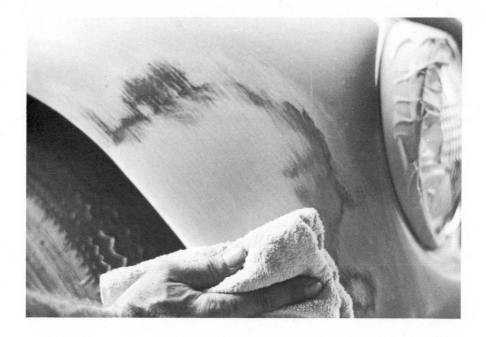

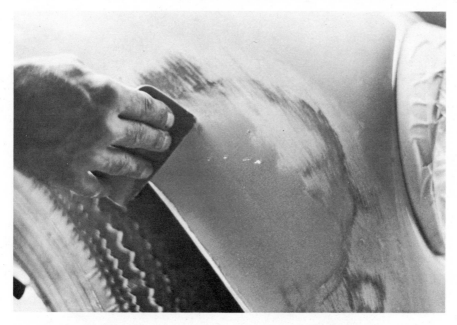

Step 8. Wipe area with clean rag (above) and recoat (below).

Step 9. Use your file as soon as the plastic becomes solid.

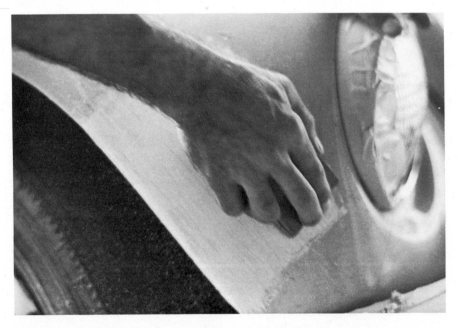

Step 10. Work the plastic down to within a hair of the desired height.

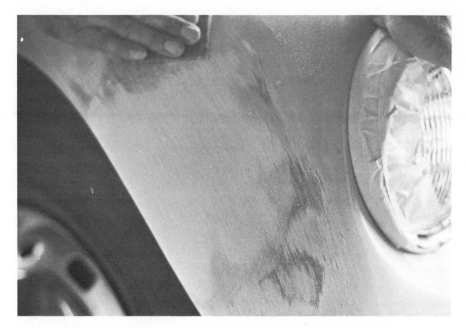

Step 11. Finish sanding with a piece of 80-grit folded in thirds. Use long smooth strokes.

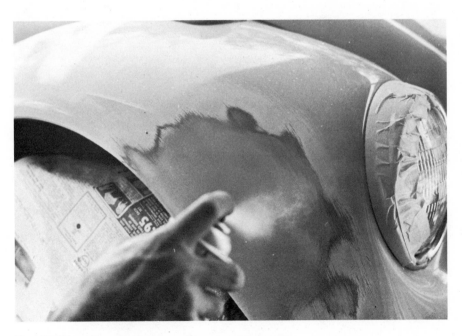

Step 12. Prime the repair area with a medium coat.

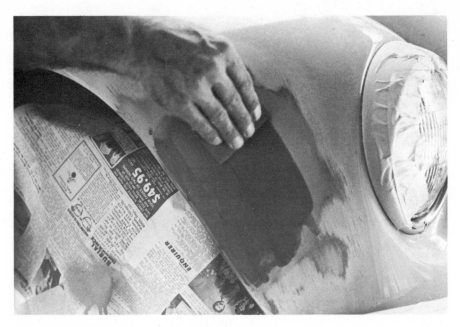

Step 13. Apply glazing putty with a squeegee.

Step 14. After the glazing has dried, block sand with the paint paddle and 100-grit paper.

Step 15. Finish sanding with a piece of 100-grit paper folded in thirds.

Step 16. Clean the entire area with a clean rag.

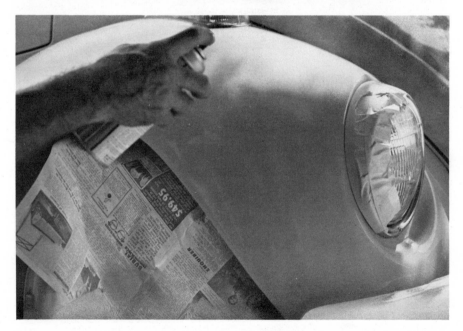

Step 17. Reprime the entire area, going out over the old finish edge to prevent rusting until you have it painted.

REPAIR 2
Creased Panel and Door Edge

A little crease behind the door is easily fixed with the dent puller. A repair procedure consisting of only fifteen steps will restore your car's beauty.

Step 1. Evaluate damage.

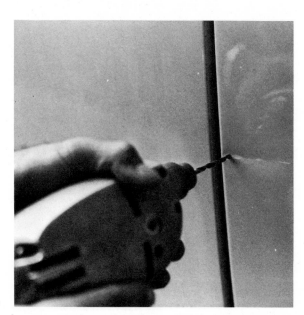

Step 2. Drill holes
along the stress line.

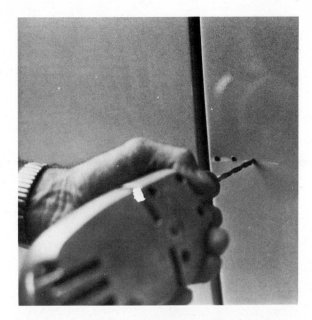

Step 3. Holes should be spaced one inch apart.

Step 4. Use the dent puller to bring the panel back to its original shape.

Step 5. Several light taps in each hole will keep the panel even. If it is still too low, repeat the step.

Step 6. Grind the old
finish back.

Step 7. With old finish
ground away (right),
apply first coat of
plastic (below).

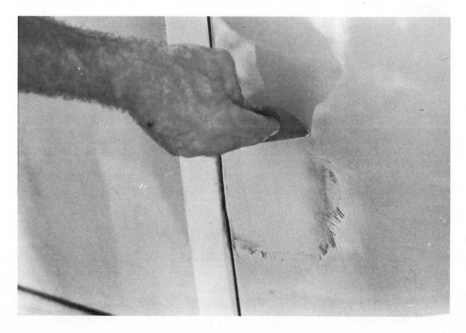

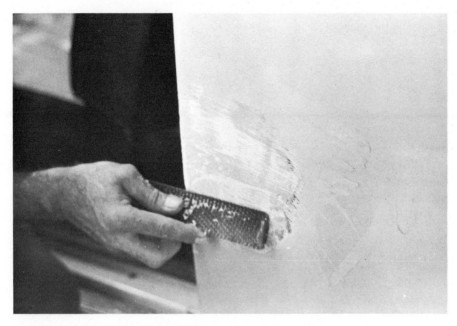

Step 8. File off any high spots as soon as the plastic becomes solid.

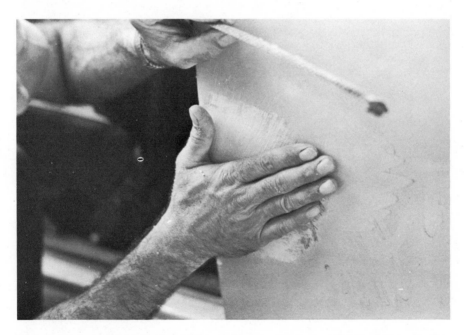

Step 9. Think straight. Find the highs and lows with your most valuable tool — the hand.

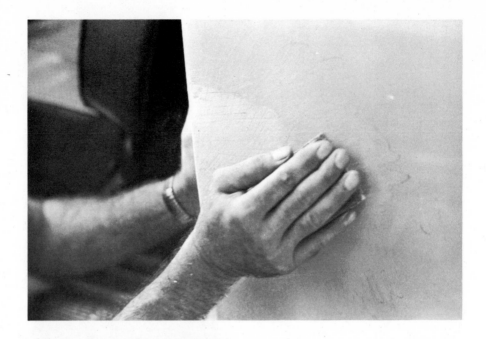

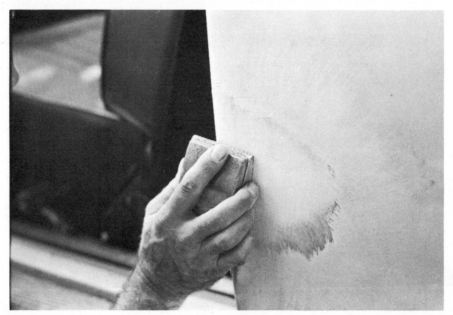

Step 10. Work the plastic down with the appropriate sanding tool.

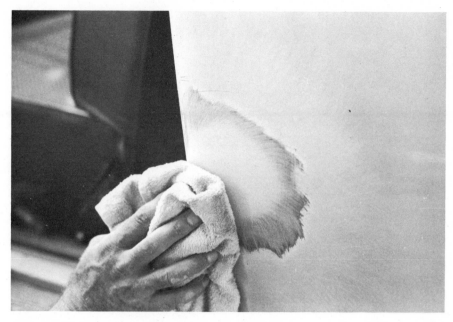

Step 11. Wipe the repair area clean with a rag.

Step 12. Prime the area with a medium coat.

Step 13. Glaze with putty and squeegee.

Step 14. Block sand the area with 100-grit paper and paddle.

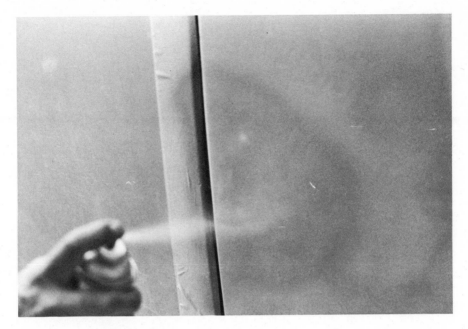

Step 15. Prime the entire area.

REPAIR 3
Crumpled Rear Quarter Panel

At first glance, this Oldsmobile Toronado quarter panel looks like a job for the body shop. Not so. By patiently and carefully following the instructions you can repair it yourself.

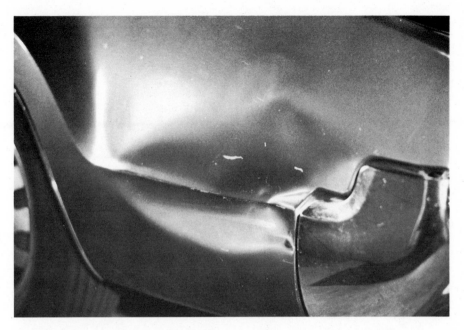

This job looks bad, but is really simple if you think it out and proceed slowly.

Step 1. Study the damage. Look at the other side of the car and study the lines of the undamaged panel.

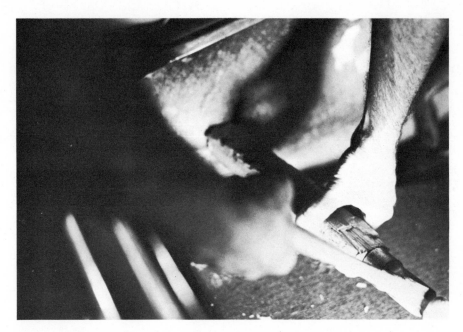

Step 2. Return the panel to its original position by tapping it out with a block of wood and a hammer.

This job was easier because access to the back side of the panel was possible through the trunk.

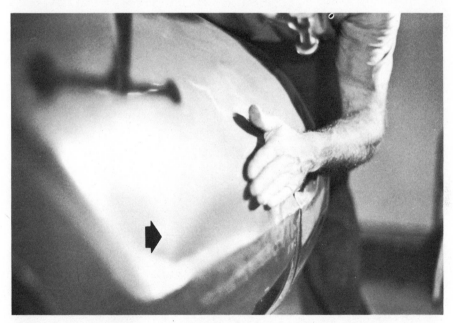

Step 3. Shape the panel. When a panel is hit this hard, you not only have low areas with a small dent, but you also have high spots (arrows). Work these down as you bring the panel back into position.

Step 4. On large areas like this, use a yardstick to locate highs and lows and check body lines.

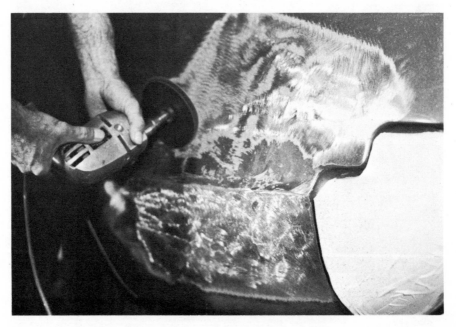

Step 5. Grind off the old finish. After grinding, you may find small areas that are still not right. Correct them now.

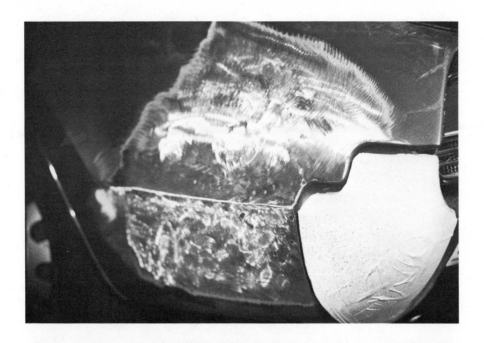

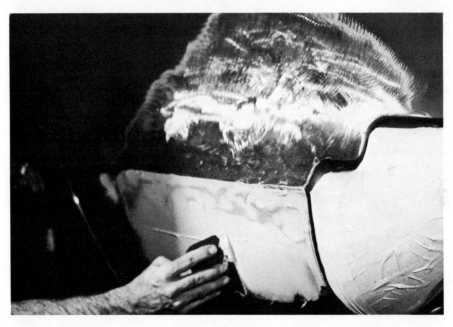

Step 6. With the finish ground back (above), tin the metal with small amounts of plastic on a spreader (below).

Step 7. Spread the plastic as smoothly as possible.

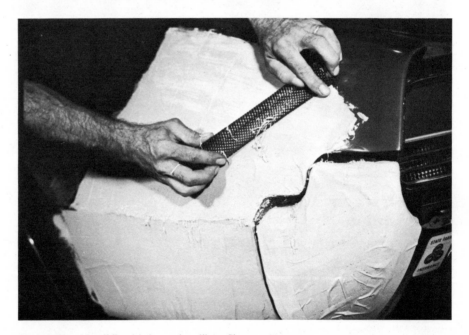

Step 8. Knock off the high spots with a file.

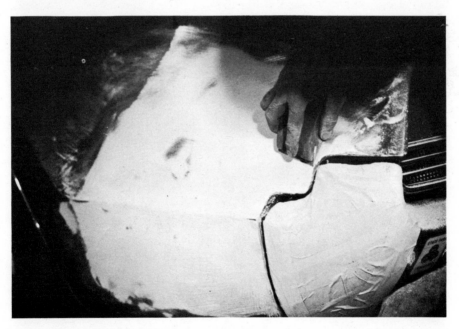

Step 9. Work the plastic down with a sanding board and block.

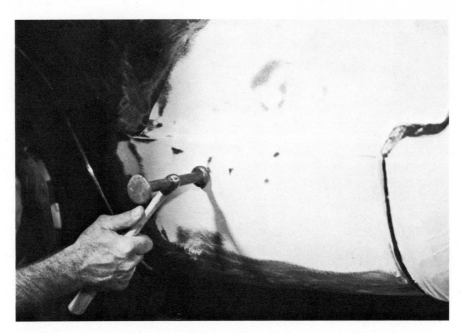

Step 10. High spots in the metal will become apparent as you sand. These can be tapped down with a body hammer before the next coat is applied.

Step 11. On a curve such as this body line, a piece of 17 in. × 2⅔ in. (36-grit) sandpaper rolled into a tube shape does a great job.

Step 12. Use the yardstick to be sure the lines are shaping up correctly and to show highs and lows.

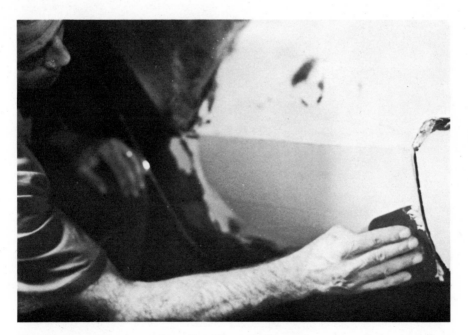

Step 13. Recoat the area. Keep the low areas in mind.

Step 14. Knock off any high spots with the file.

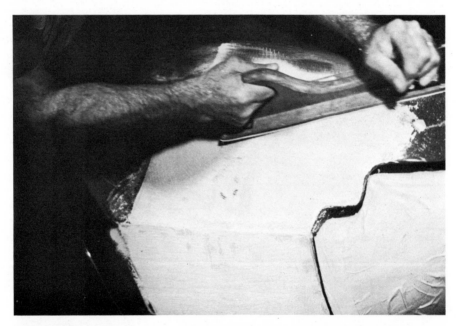

Step 15. Work the plastic down with sanding board and block. If a third and fourth application are needed, don't feel bad.

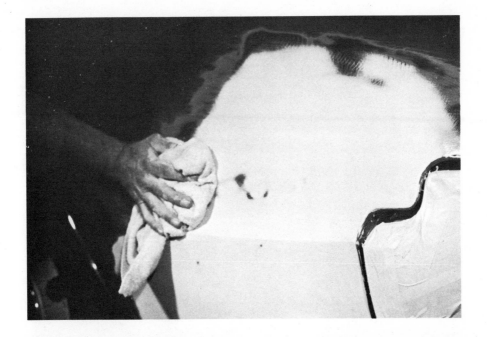

Step 16. When you have the desired surface, wipe it with a rag (above), and prime it with a medium coat of primer (below).

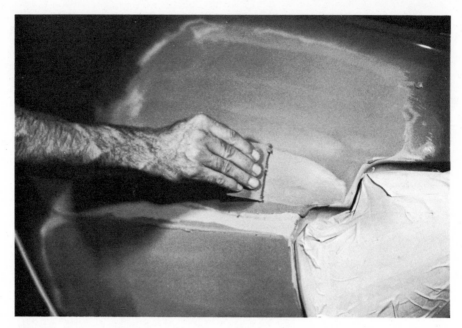

Step 17. Glaze the area in one-stroke applications.

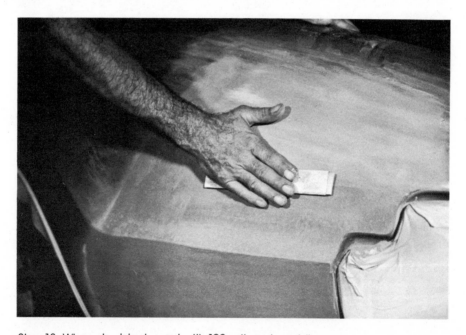

Step 18. When dry, block sand with 100-grit and paddle.

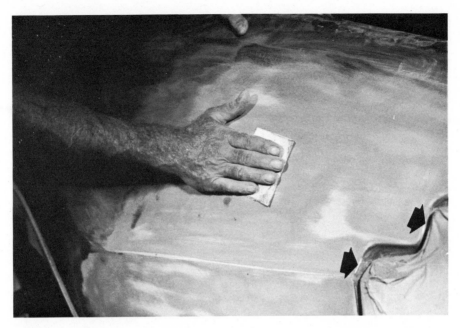

Step 19. Finish-sand with 100-grit folded in thirds. Use long, light, even strokes. Be sure edges are straight, and don't allow excess material to build up (arrows).

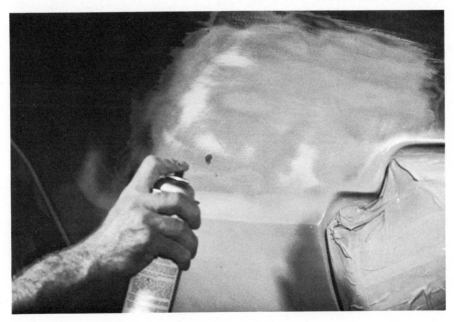

Step 20. Prime the entire area, being sure that all bare metal is covered.

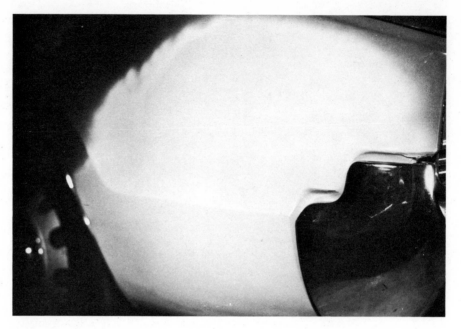

The finished product. This job would save you about $90.

REPAIR 4

Damaged Door
and Front
Quarter Panel

You parked your Dodge Dart on the street overnight and woke up to this mess the next morning? This type of scratch or gouge and dent damage is repaired with the dent puller, using the filler techniques.

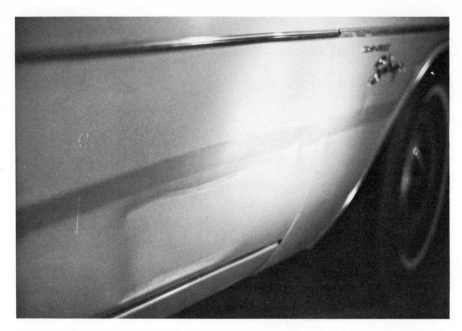

This looks like another rough job, but with a little patience you can easily do it at home.

Step 1. Study the stress lines, and drill the dent puller holes.

Step 2. Work the panel gradually back into position. As you are using the dent puller, watch what the rest of the panel is doing.

Step 3. Use the palm of the hand to find highs and lows. Work them out as you go.

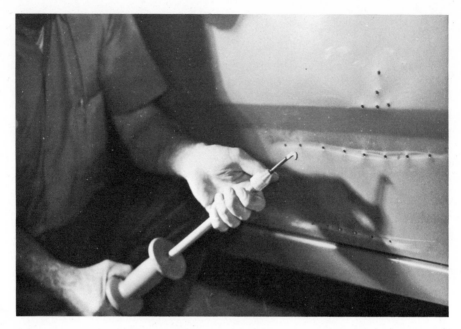

This body hook tool is very handy and comes with some dent pullers. It is used when you can get behind the edge of the damaged panel.

Step 4. The edge of this fender is easily brought out to the proper position with the body hook.

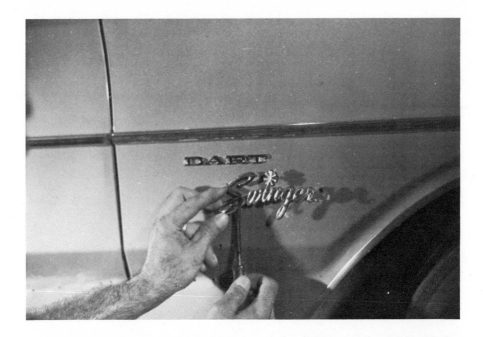

Step 5. Most emblems are fastened to the body by means of barrel type fasteners. (above and below). They are easily removed with a small screwdriver.

Step 6. This is the latest type of side molding. It is easily replaced with a good trim adhesive.

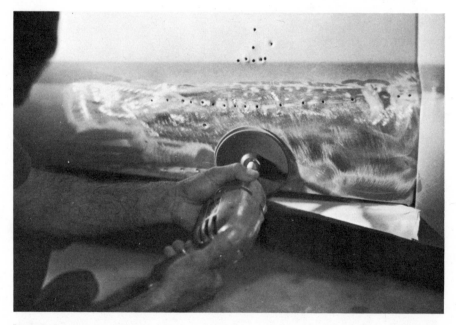

Step 7. Begin the grinding operation when you are sure the panel is as close to the original as you can get it.

Step 8. Grind the old finish well back from the damage. Notice that one panel at a time is finished. This way the plastic doesn't get too hard on one panel while you are working on another.

Step 9. Use a small wire brush for hard-to-get-at places.

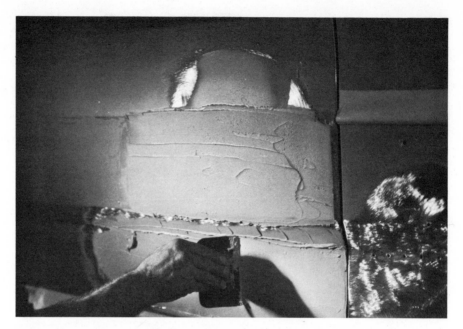

Step 10. Spread the plastic as smoothly and quickly as possible. On panels with sculptured lines such as this, concentrate on those lines first. Then do the low spots on the flat portions of the panel.

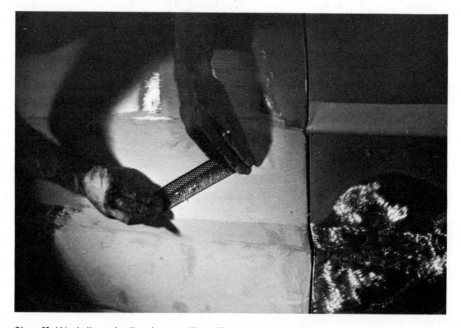

Step 11. Work the plastic down with a file as soon as it becomes solid.

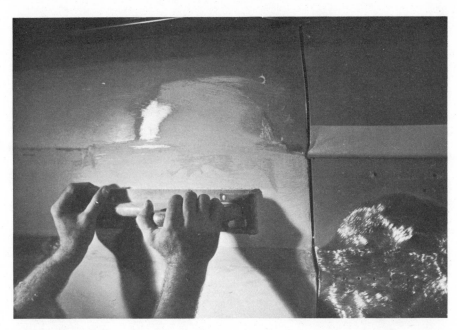

Step 12. Use a sanding board on large areas like this to obtain straight panels.

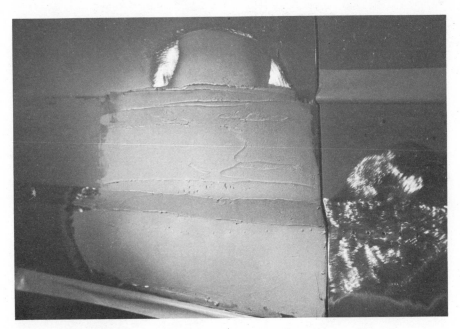

Step 13. Recoat as many times as necessary to straighten the panel.

Step 14. After the first panel is done, start on the second.

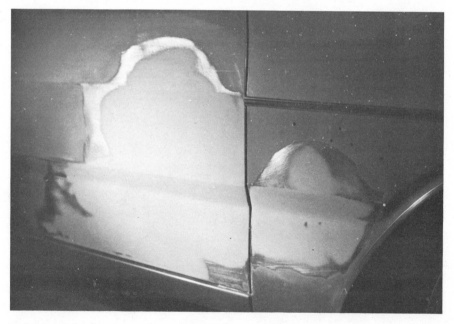

Step 15. After a few hours your panels should look like this. Prime and glaze as in the previous repairs.

REPAIRS 5 AND 6
Dented Trunk Lid and Hood

The following two repairs differ only in that the panels are functional. The hood and the trunk lid, or deck lid as it is sometimes called, open and shut so in addition to straightening the sheet metal skin, you have to align the panel so that it fits squarely in the opening it covers. Don't panic now, for it is really a simple operation. As in the previous jobs, take your time and think the problem out.

Whenever you are working on a hood panel or deck lid, follow these simple basic steps.

1. Straighten the dent or damage that has been done to the panel by pulling or knocking it out to the tolerances mentioned in the previous repairs.
2. When the dent is roughed out and *before* you apply the plastic filler, align the panel so it fits the opening properly. There are several adjustments that can be made here. Though they seem impossible at first, take your time and follow the step-by-step photos.

3. When you have the dent roughed out and the panel aligned properly in the opening, apply your filler as you did before. The only other difference with these panels (hoods and trunk lids) is that they are very visible to anyone looking at or driving the car. So do an extra special job so that your work is sure not to show. The best compliment any body man can be paid is for someone to say, "You can never notice his work."

One word of caution here for safety's sake. Upon repairing the hood panel, check the hood latch assembly. If there is any damage or if the latch doesn't seem to work well, go to the dealer and buy a new unit. Many a hood latch has been repaired just enough to get by only to have the hood fly open at high speed, creating all kinds of havoc. Don't take the chance to save the low price of a new latch assembly.

The same problem exists with the trunk latch assembly. It is not likely to become a life and death situation, but if you try to repair a trunk latch that should really be replaced, you may find yourself unable to get into your trunk. This could be really frustrating after a thirty-mile drive to your favorite fishing spot when you find you can't get to your fishing gear on the inside. *Replace latches that appear to be bad.*

Repair 5 is on a trunk lid which was hit just above the bumper. Follow the proper steps in repairing it. Pull out the dent, align the lid in the opening and metal finish the dent.

Arrow shows how the impact knocked the lid out of alignment.

The same deck lid at another angle. Note the trunk lid-body seam. When properly aligned, this seam will be even.

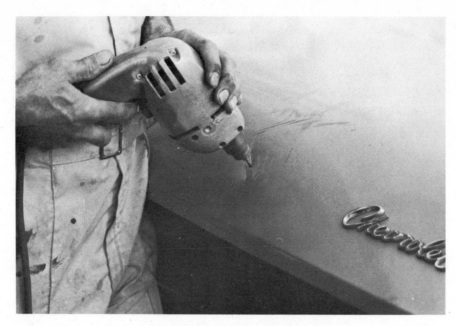

Step 1. Before attempting to align the lid, rough out the dent. This will remove any unseen stress in the lid. Make your holes for the puller with a drill.

Step 2. Bring the lid panel back to its original position with the puller.

Step 3. Grind back the old finish.

Step 4. Before applying plastic filler, align the lid in the opening. Arrows show the adjustment direction.

After the lid is properly aligned, the seams will be even.

Step 5. In cases where the leading edge of the lid is too high or too low, you will have to bend the hinges. To lower the leading edge (front of lid), simply open the trunk lid fully and then force it up.

Step 6. To raise the leading edge of the trunk lid, use a wooden block as shown and force the lid down. Do one side at a time. The hinge will bend at the arrow.

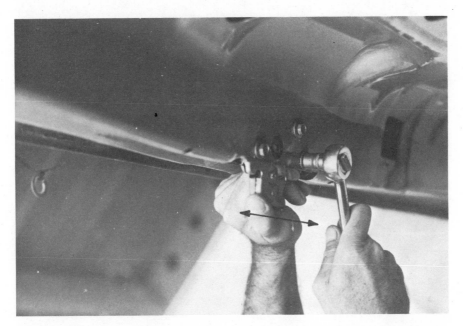

Step 7. To raise or lower the rear edge of the lid, simply adjust the latch mechanism. On this model, the latch assembly is in the lid and adjusts from side to side. The striker is on the rear body panel. The arrows show direction of adjustment. On some cars, the adjustment locations are reversed.

Step 8. Once the lid is aligned properly, apply filler and work it down as in the previous repairs.

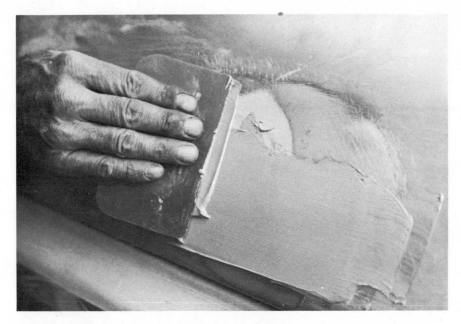

Step 9. Spread the plastic smoothly and quickly.

Step 10. Block sand the plastic with a rubber block or sanding board.

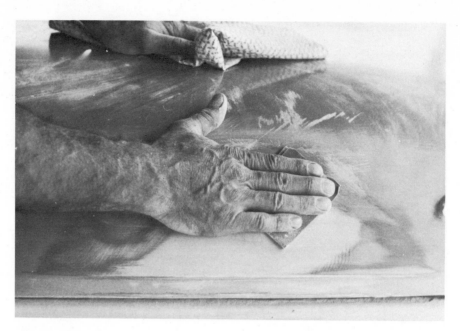

Step 11. Just before priming, sand the area smooth with a piece of 80-grit in the palm of the hand.

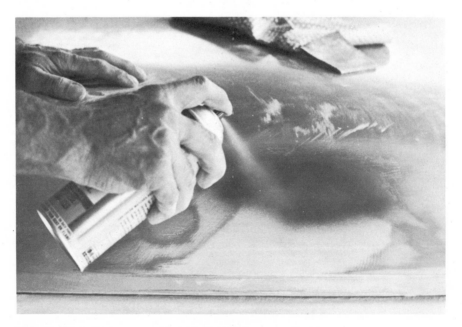

Step 12. Prime the area as in previous repairs.

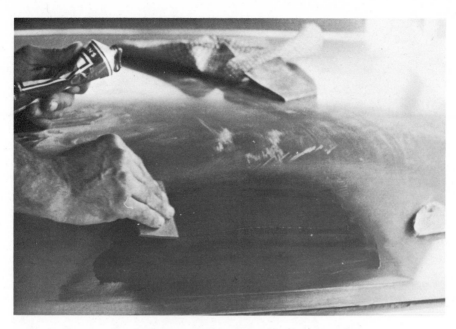

Step 13. After the primer dries, coat the area with glazing putty.

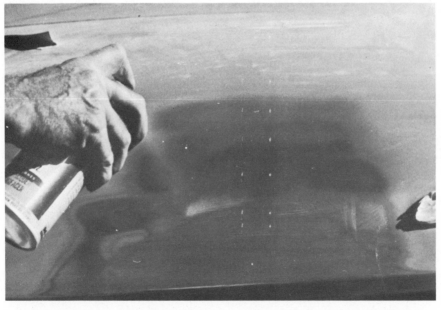

Step 14. After the putty dries and you have it blocked off with paint paddle and 220-grit, prime the entire area to prevent rust until you can have it painted.

Repair 6 involves the hood panel. This panel was hit in the right front knocking it out of alignment.

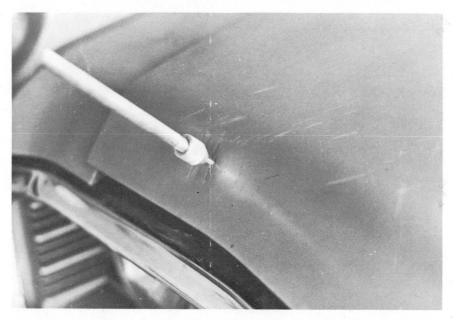

Step 1. First straighten the dent by drilling holes and pulling it out with the dent puller.

Step 2. Grind the old finish back.

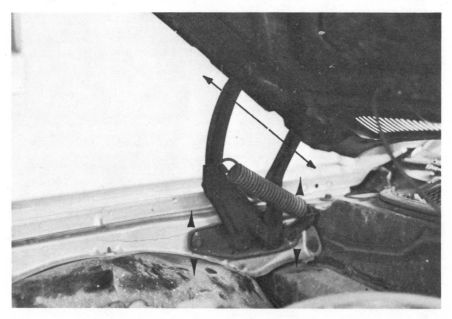

Step 3. Before you apply any plastic, align the hood in the opening. There are usually four bolts on each hinge. The two bolts holding the hood to the hinge adjust the hood forward and back. The two bolts that hold the hinge to the fender control the height of the rear edge of the hood.

Once the hood is properly aligned, the hood-fender seams should look like this.

Step 4. Hood height is adjusted as shown. Turn the lock shaft clockwise to lower the front of the hood. Turn counterclockwise to raise the front of the hood.

Step 5. Be sure the hood latch is operating properly. A bad hood latch is dangerous. When the hood is fitting and operating properly, you can metal finish the damaged area as in the previous repairs and be ready for the painter.

Preparing Your Car for a New Paint Job

As I've said before, unless you are prepared to spend hundreds of dollars on special equipment, don't try to do the actual spray painting yourself. This applies doubly when the car is to get a complete paint job. However, if you get the car ready to paint at home, you can (1) get a perfect job because you can take all the time you need to get it right, and (2) save yourself about two-thirds of the cost of a new paint job. What most people don't know is that most of the high cost of completely refinishing an automobile is the labor of preparing it for spraying. The actual time it takes to spray a car is only about one-half hour. So . . . if your car is destined for a bright, new, shiny finish, roll up your sleeves and let's get started. If you follow the simple procedures and take your time to do it right, you can stand back and look at a beautiful finished product.

There are four basic steps to follow when completely refinishing an auto.

1. Pre-clean the complete body from bumper to bumper with a good pre-cleaning solvent.

2. Feather-edge all nicks, scratches and slight imperfections in the old finish. If you have done any body work using this book as a guide, then all of the old finish edges that were ground back must be feather-edged at this time. Spot prime all these areas and block sand them with a paint paddle and 220-grit open face sandpaper.

3. Sand the complete car with 320-grit open face sandpaper.

4. Using masking tape and newspaper, tape off all areas that are not to be painted such as bumpers, moldings, glass, etc.

The following instructions for preparing your car for refinishing include many professional techniques so that the finished product will be nothing short of perfect. In doing this though, I have tried to use language that the layman might very easily understand. There is only one way to do a job, and that way is, of course, the right way. Otherwise the material you purchase and the time and energy you spend will be wasted.

List of Supplies Needed

This list of supplies includes everything you will need to prepare your car for refinishing. They can be purchased at any auto supply or auto paint supply store, and most large discount stores. When you buy these supplies, do not purchase the paint. The paint is supplied by the shop that is going to apply the finish. The reason for this is that different painters use different brands. They are used to their favorite brand and do their best work with it, so let them buy the paint. You will need:

One gallon of pre-cleaning solvent. (6)
Two or three wooden paint paddles. (2)
Three rolls of ¾-in. masking tape. (1)
Twelve sheets of 220-grit open face sandpaper. (3)
Twelve sheets of 320-grit open face sandpaper. (4)
One or two spray cans of lacquer base primer. (5)

Don't over-buy on these items, as you can always go back for more if you run out.

Step 1
Pre-cleaning the Body

The very first step in preparing the car for refinishing is to remove all foreign substances from the old finish, including wax, road tars,

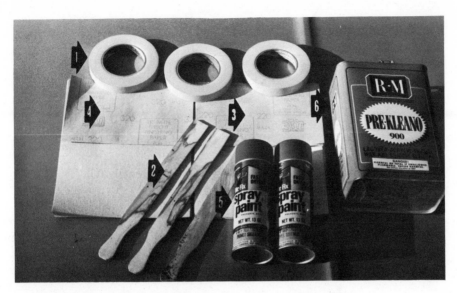

Materials needed to prepare your car for a new paint job.

tree sap, etc. They must be completely removed to insure that the new paint film will completely adhere to the old finish.

For this job you need a good pre-cleaning solvent. Before you use this solvent, read the label and do exactly as it says with no short cuts. This is a very important step if you expect your new

This high contrast photo shows the wet area when using the pre-cleaner. Do about 12 square inches at a time. Apply the cleaner, and while the area is still wet, wipe dry.

finish to last. I always do one panel at a time, such as a complete fender, so as not to miss a spot accidentally that could give me trouble later. Most pre-cleaner labels will tell you to wipe an area with solvent on a clean rag and, while the surface is still wet, wipe it dry with a clean rag. I'm sure you have already figured out the reason why. Yes, the rag dampened with the solvent loosens the foreign substance and the clean dry rag wipes it from the old finish. This leaves it clean and ready for the following operations. Change rags often. When you are certain you have done this first step completely, you are ready to move on to Step 2.

Step 2
Feather-edging and Spot Priming-block Sanding

The second step is feather-edging the old finish wherever it is broken or interrupted; for example, a stone bruise or a nick where someone has opened a car door into the side of your car, etc. You must also feather-edge any areas where you have done any body work and have ground the old finish back to make room for your metal finishing. The reason for this is very obvious if you think about it for a moment. First of all, think of the old finish as having some degree of thickness. A coat of paint is only a film covering the metal, but it does, in fact, have thickness. Any interruptions, such as scratches or chips, will cause a hole in the film. If you were to cover this hole in the old finish with a coat of bright shiny paint, it would be highlighted.

What you have to do is build the hole or low area back up to the level of the old finish with primer. Sand the area of the hole to taper the abrupt edge of the hole gradually out to the level of the old finish. When this is done, simply spot prime a couple of times and, when dry, block sand with 220-grit sandpaper and a paint paddle. Feel the area with the flat of your hand. If it is perfectly smooth, go on to the next area. If you still feel a slight low spot, prime it again and block it down when dry.

The illustrations show such nicks and scratches and just how they are treated. It is really as simple as A B C.

A. Feather-edge the hole or scratch in the old finish with 220-grit paper and paddle so that it gradually tapers out to the level of the old finish.
B. Spot spray with lacquer-type primer, two or three coats, allowing each coat to dry before applying the next one.
C. Block sand with the 220-grit paper and paddle when the primer is dry.

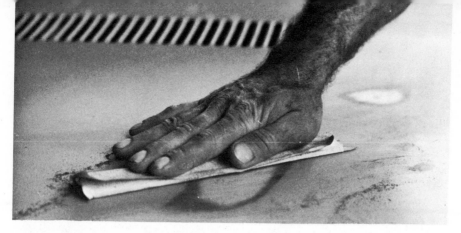

Feather-edging a typical nick or hole in the old finish with 220-grit and paint paddle.

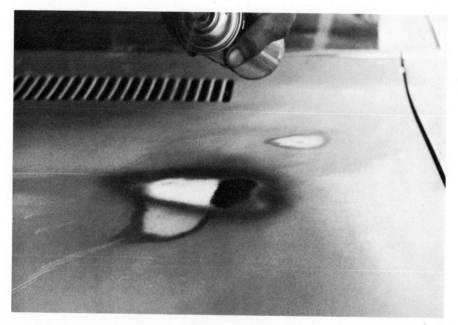

Priming the area just feather-edged to bring the void up to the level of the old finish.

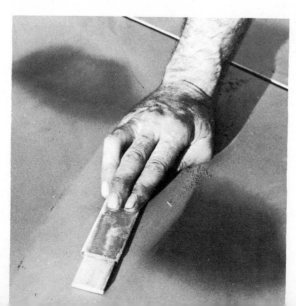

Block sanding with the same 220-grit paper and paddle. If the void can still be felt, repeat the operation.

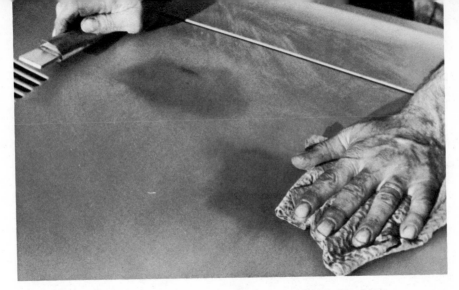

When properly done, the finish should be smooth and look like this.

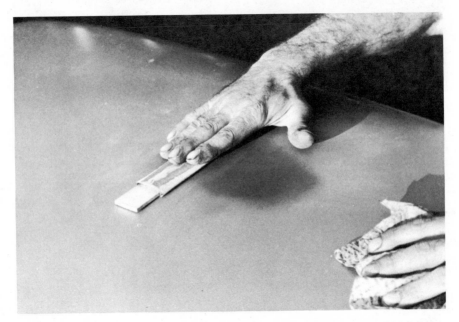

The same treatment is given to all holes, nicks and scratches in the old finish. Feather-edge the bad spot, prime, and block sand to make the area level with the old finish.

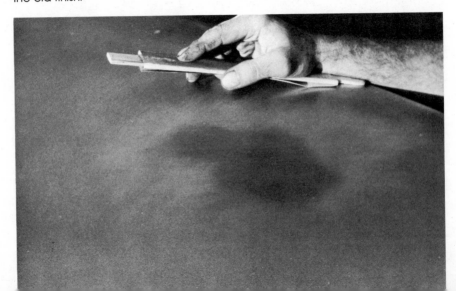

A good example of scratches in the old finish.

Feather-edge the scratches with 220-grit and paddle.

Properly feather-edged, the scratched area should look like this.

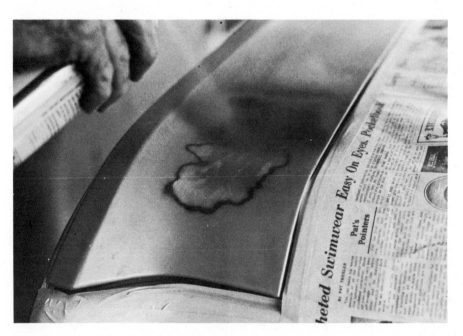

Temporarily mask off the area and prime it.

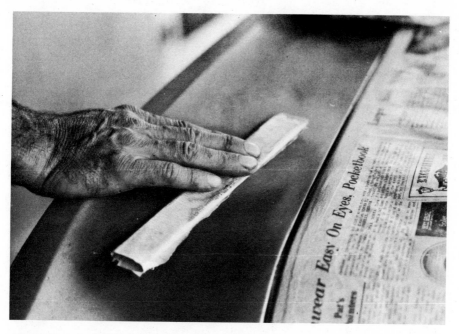

After primer is dry, block sand the area. If you can still feel the void, repeat the operation.

If you've made any body repairs, these must also be feather-edged.

Repaired areas should look like this before priming.

Prime all metal finished areas after feather-edging.

When primer has dried, block sand with 220-grit and paddle. If the area is still not smooth, reprime and block sand again. Keep repeating this operation until the area is smooth and you can feel no imperfections with the palm of your hand.

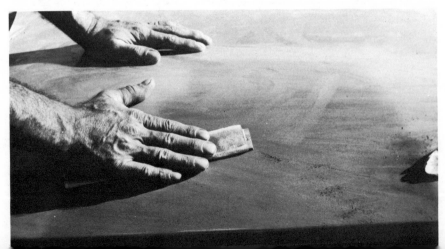

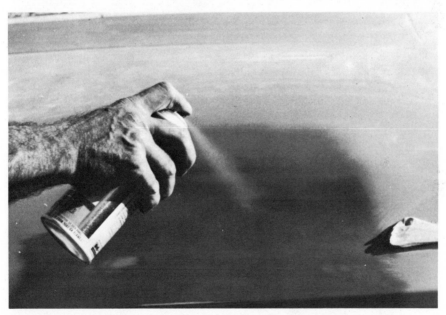

The area is primed again, since portions of metal and filler show through. It will be sanded again when you sand the complete car.

I've talked about doing a job and doing it well, without taking any shortcuts. Well, here is a short cut to certain failure, one I have seen many times, both in professional shops and on do-it-yourself jobs. Instead of going through the sand and prime operation step-by-step, glazing putty is wiped into these small imperfections and when dry, leveled off with the old finish. This sounds easy doesn't it? It is, but that glob of filler that is wiped into the hole in the old finish is destined to become a *pop-out*. It will do just that, pop-out and take the paint that is covering it along. Presto, you have a shiny new paint job with a hole in it.

The reason this method doesn't work is very simple. When you feather-edge the damage in the old finish, tapering the abrupt edge gradually out to the level of the old finish, and apply primer, it becomes a part of the film covering the metal. When one stuffs a gob of putty in the hole, it is not a part of the film, as it has definite edges. It becomes only a sort of plug or insert in the old finish. When the new paint is applied, with all it's "chemical hotness," the putty or filler becomes soft and sooner or later is dislodged. This, of course, leaves you with the same hole.

A similar process is used for a large area such as one that you have repaired. The edge of the old finish has to be gradually feather-edged and the metal finished area has to be built up with primer and then the entire area block sanded with a paint paddle and 220-grit sandpaper. Once these damaged areas in the old finish are taken care of, you are ready to go on to Step 3. Be certain to do a good job on Step 2. This is where most do-it-yourselfers fail.

Step 3
Sanding the Complete Car

Step 3, sanding the complete car, is another project that should be done panel-by-panel. Do one panel completely before going on to the next. This step is the next-to-most-tedious part of preparing to refinish, but it is, in fact, just about the most important. The better you do this step, the better the finish you're going to end up with, and most important, the longer it will hold up.

Take a sheet of 320-grit open face sandpaper and fold it in half from the top to the bottom. Crease it, and tear the paper in half. Take one of the halves and fold it in thirds. This gives you a good sized piece for palming. Start sanding on any panel, sanding in straight lines back and forth. As the paper tends to build up with sanding dust, knock it against your free hand to reduce clogging. Sand an area about twelve inches square until the old finish is completely dull and you feel no imperfections as you run your hand over your work. The reason for sanding until the old finish is completely dull is to insure complete bonding of the new finish. Of course, you are feeling with your free hand to detect any small nicks or foreign matter that might be in the old finish.

You're now ready to sand the complete car with 320-grit paper and lots of patience.

Tear the sandpaper in half, and then fold each half in thirds.

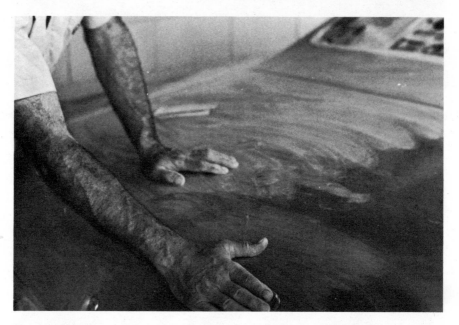

Sand in straight lines back and fourth in an area about twelve inches square. Sand until the old finish is completely smooth and dull. Sand over all the areas that were primed as well. Be sure all the scratches and imperfections are sanded out on these areas.

Continue until the entire car is sanded. Care must be taken to sand every square inch of your car's sheet metal, right up to the very edge of moldings, door handles, hood emblems, etc. If you are having trouble sanding close to the edge of these items without scratching them, tape them over temporarily to protect them. If rust appears to be creeping out from under any of these trim pieces, it may be best to remove them. When you have them off, you can sand the finish down to bare metal and prime as in the feather-edging process. Otherwise, do not remove these items and disturb their factory installation. Getting in close to items like windshield wiper shafts where they go through the cowl, door handles, door locks, etc. is very time consuming, but very necessary to prevent your new paint job from peeling in just a few months, so do it. Sand the entire surface no matter how hard it is to get at, if you want a top-flight professional job. On the feather-edged areas and the areas that you repaired, continue to sand just as you are sanding the rest of the car. Look closely at these areas for grinder marks and coarse sandpaper scratches.

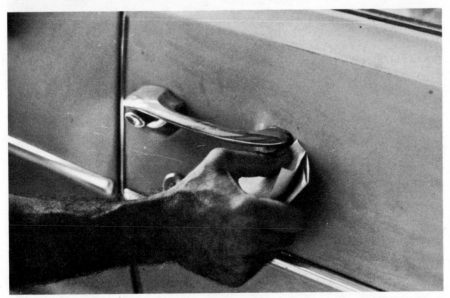

When sanding the complete car, be careful to sand right up to the very edge of moldings and door handles. If you don't, the paint will soon peel from these areas.

Here are two areas that are hard to get at, but they must be sanded if you want a good paint job.

If you sand through to bare metal, reprime that area and work around that spot until it dries. Then go back and sand it again. Usually, you won't be able to feel these marks in the primer. You have to look closely for them, and they must be sanded out. If they are not taken care of they will show in the finished product.

When you have sanded the whole car, just to be sure of your work, go back and check the areas that were feather-edged and primed and any areas that were repaired. These are trouble spots that can ruin an otherwise good job. When you have double-checked your work and are satisfied with it, you have completed Step 3. Just in case I should happen to walk up behind you, better check it over once more. I'm awful fussy.

Step 4
Masking the Car

This is a fairly simple operation but is probably the most tedious. If it is done quickly, items like chrome moldings, emblems, window glass will get paint on them and look thoroughly shabby when the job is finished. A poorly masked car is the result of amateur work. There is no set rule for masking, as we all do it differently. The end result is the important factor.

1. All items that are not to receive paint must be completely masked with tape and/or paper. This includes windows, bumpers, and vinyl tops. Be as neat as possible. Avoid pockets in the paper where dust can gather and cause a dirty finished product.
2. For safety's sake, no windows or lights of any kind should be masked until the car is driven to the shop that will do the painting. If the car is to be driven some distance to the shop, don't paper the grille or the car may overheat. Don't expect the painter to do it though or the price will go up! Do it yourself when you have the car at the shop.
3. Do not mask until a day or two before taking the car to the shop. The longer masking tape stays on the car the harder it will be to get off. Don't let the car get wet once you start masking. Water can get trapped and then blown out on the finish as the painter is applying the paint.

Taping a door handle. It is better to leave a small part of the handle exposed than to get too close to the body and possibly pull the fresh paint off when you untape the car.

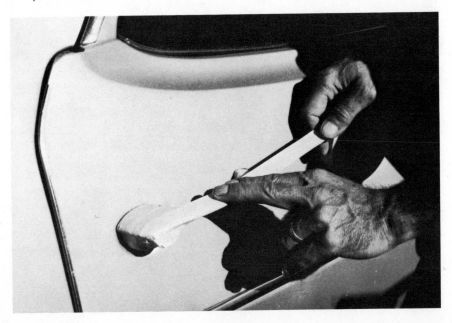

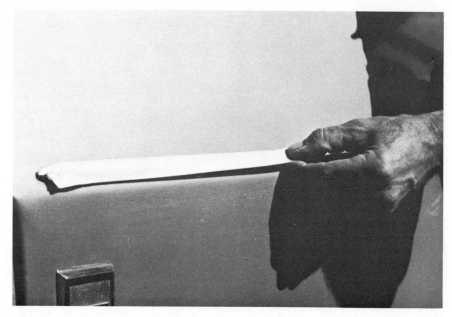

Tape mouldings in the same manner as door handles. Be sure that the tape doesn't touch the body.

A typical masked section. Notice that all taping is neat and orderly.

The pen reminds you not to get any tape on any part of the sheet metal to be painted. Naturally, when you untape the car that portion under the tape wouldn't have any paint on it.

Taping is a time-consuming job, but it must be done. Some emblems can be removed and some can't. Take your time and do it right.

When taping an antenna, don't spiral the tape. Instead, tape the length of the unit. It will be much easier to untape.

When taping the windows, be very neat and avoid pockets and folds in the paper that can trap dirt and cause a dirty final product. CAUTION: Do not tape windows or lights until car is at the paint shop.

By now you should be just about ready for the painter. If you haven't already lined up a shop, call around to do your pricing rather than taking the car around to different shops. Remember, like all services we pay for today, price is not the only consideration. After all the work you've just done, quality is equally important. Ask around about different shops. Ask your friends or call the Better Business Bureau. Be sure of the shop that is going to do the painting.

When you talk to the man at the shop, say, "I have prepared my car for painting and would like to know how much you charge for applying a sealer coat and spraying the paint."

Be sure they are planning to seal your old finish before they paint, as sealing is important for good adhesion, good gloss, and good coverage of any minor imperfections you may have missed. Good luck to you, and congratulations on a great job!

Man, doesn't that baby look fine?

Care and Maintenance of a New Finish

After your car is repainted, put back any items you removed prior to painting such as moldings or emblems. For the next thirty days be very careful of the new finish, as it will be soft and quite vulnerable to nicks and scratches. Keep the car out of the hot sun as much as possible, and keep the finish free of dirt. To wash the car for the first two weeks, just rinse it off with clear water from a garden hose and wipe it dry with a clean, soft cloth. After two weeks you may wash the car with clean, soft rags and a mild soap solution. Be sure the soap is mild! Do not use harsh detergents!

Do not wax the car for at least thirty days, as the new finish has to breathe in order to dry properly. When you wax the car, use a good brand of paste wax. They are harder to apply and polish to be sure, but they last longer and do a better job of protecting the finish from the elements.

By the way, there is someone at your door. I think it is the guy who lives across the street. He probably wants you to fix his quarter panel. Good luck.

Your Shop Foreman
ROBERT HARMAN

Glossary

Block Sanding   Using a flat object and sandpaper to obtain a flat surface.

Glazing   Using special surface putty to fill minor low areas and sandpaper marks.

Hardener   Chemical that is added to plastic filler to induce hardening.

Metal Finishing   Straightening a damaged panel with hammer, dent puller, etc., before applying filler.

Metal Stretch   The displacement of a formed panel by impact.

Mudding a Panel   Applying plastic filler.

Mud-slinger   Modern-day body man. (That's you, from now on.)

Pin Holes   An unwanted characteristic of plastic fillers, usually caused by improper mixing of the material.

Spot Glazing   Filling pin holes and minor imperfections in a nearly finished panel.

Stress Lines   Low areas in a damaged panel that usually start at the actual point of impact and travel outward.

Index